The author has made an editorial decision to create the plural of "Jesus" as "Jesus'." This deviates slightly from the traditional style of "Jesus's."

Designed by Joyce Teo

Paperback ISBN 978-0-578-72936-7

THE Be-Attitude DEVOTIONAL

Finding Greatness Through His Heart

For NiKKi,
May you be richly blessed by your time w/ Him
Katherine

dedication

I am dedicating this book to my family and friends. Thank you for believing in me when I didn't even believe in myself.

I am dedicating this book to all the women who have a true desire to find everyday greatness through the heart of Jesus.

HOW TO USE THIS JOURNAL

Hello, sweet friend,

Thanks for picking up this devotional. I know it wasn't by coincidence. This monthly devotional is designed to tackle specific attitudes in the Christian walk and help you draw closer to God. Numerous studies show that it takes twenty-one days to break a habit. My prayer is that in thirty days, you will develop a new habit. This monthly entry includes a devotional passage, reflection questions, Scripture study, and personal journal entry pages. Be blessed as you journey toward creating a life of greatness through the heart of God.

God bless you in your journey,

Katherine Brey

be intentional

An unintentional life accepts everything and does nothing.
An intentional life embraces only the things that will add to the mission of significance.

— JOHN C. MAXWELL

Intentional living is the art of making our own choices before others' choices make us.

— RICHIE NORTON

In a day and age when people often operate on autopilot, we must focus on the discipline of intentionality. The invention of the internet has made it simple to follow a template for everything. Unfortunately, our journey in life has no template as we were all created uniquely. Psalm 139:13–14 states: "I will give thanks and praise to You, for I am fearfully and wonderfully made; wonderful are Your works, and my soul knows it very well" (AMP).

Our uniqueness requires us to progress with intent toward our relationship with God, ourselves, and others. The achievement of goals and fulfillment of dreams necessitate intentionality. I am reminded of the woman with the issue of blood in Matthew 9:20–22. Imagine the conversation she had with herself that morning after years and years of this debilitating disease. She probably heard of Jesus' fame, of his healing, provision, and deliverance. She was stirred up at the idea that he might help. She was a woman on a mission, intent on touching his garment and receiving her healing.

We often think that intentionality must be pursued with grand gestures or full speed ahead, and yet the woman with the issue of blood had neither. Her goal was not even to touch his hand but just the hem of his garment. Just a tiny touch of the corner of his robe was all she desired. How often do we miss out on God's best because we do not persist in small measures? I am reminded of the Scripture in Zechariah 4:10: "Do not despise these small beginnings, for the Lord rejoices to see the work begin, to see the plumb line in Zerubbabel's hand" (NLT).

What a monumental task it must have been when the returning exiles were faced with rebuilding the temple. They wanted to quit even before they started, and the prophet Zechariah had to encourage them to intently begin and stay the course despite all the obstacles before them.

Marie Sklodowska, a remarkable woman known to the world by her married name, Marie Curie, left an indelible mark in history. She was recognized for her passionate pursuit in the fields of chemistry and biology at a time when it was unusual for her gender to even express a slight interest in those subjects. Undeterred, disciplined, and intentional, she advanced in both academic arenas and discovered two unknown elements: radium and polonium. The recipient of two Nobel Peace Prizes, Marie not only embarked in unchartered waters for her time but also laid the foundation for others to build upon. Despite becoming a widow and raising two children alone, she exuded intentionality, setting an example for her daughters to never give up, regardless of opposition. Her daughter, Irene Joliot-Curie, along with her husband, went on to win a Nobel Prize, no doubt inspired by her mother who paved the way.[1]

What about you? Have you talked yourself out of accomplishing an especially important task because you have not been intentional? Have you been living life on autopilot? Or have you been living with intentionality?

____

____

____

____

____

____

Prayer: Dear heavenly Father, I ask from this moment forward that I would pursue your will for my life with intent. I repent of any lackadaisical attitude toward even the smallest of areas in my life and for taking for granted any small intentional measure to achieve what you have laid before me. I quiet my soul right now and invite you to speak clearly and intentionally to my heart. May I fall in love with the pursuit of intentionality, as it will draw me all the more closer to you. Amen.

STEPS I CAN TAKE TO BECOME MORE INTENTIONAL

1. ________________________________

2. ________________________________

3. ________________________________

Scripture ON BEING INTENTIONAL

> For everything there is a season, and a time for every matter under heaven:
> a time to be born, and a time to die;
> a time to plant, and a time to pluck up what is planted;
> a time to kill, and a time to heal;
> a time to break down, and a time to build up;
> a time to weep, and a time to laugh;
> a time to mourn, and a time to dance;
> a time to cast away stones, and a time to gather stones together;
> a time to embrace, and a time to refrain from embracing;
> a time to seek, and a time to lose;
> a time to keep, and a time to cast away;
> a time to tear, and a time to sew;
> a time to keep silence, and a time to speak;
> a time to love, and a time to hate;
> a time for war, and a time for peace. ~ *Ecclesiastes 3:1–8*

Week One

Week two

Week three

Week Four

ATTITUDE #2

be loving

Human love is directed to the other person for his own sake, spiritual love loves him from Christ's sake.

— DIETRICH BONHOEFFER

Of course, whenever one mentions hugs, kisses, hearts, and expressions of love, thoughts of Valentine's Day quickly rush to mind. On that day, young and old engage in acts of affection toward their sweetheart, and all is right in the world. Yet maybe it is just me, but I often wonder how the landscape of my life, my little corner of the universe, would change if I daily operated more out of the principle of love. Often, I skim over acts of love as I whiz by, focused on accomplishing my important to-do list. Acts of love are not on my radar as they should be, if I am honest. We are called to act and treat others from a place of love. This is not just a principle but a commandment and challenge from Jesus as he shared with his disciples the secret to kingdom living. The apostle John dictates Jesus' words regarding loving in John 13:34–35. "A new command I give you: Love one another. As I have loved you, so you must love one another. By this everyone will know that you are my disciples if you love one another" (NIV).

This seems like such a simple concept and yet is so difficult to implement at times. Oh, the task is easy enough when you look in your little one's eyes as you play peek-a-boo; when you are standing at the altar, soaking in dreams of the future with your Prince Charming; or watching a movie with your parents and laughing till tears stream down your face. The world can look glorious and wonderful in those times; the love flows freely and readily without effort.

We enjoy our love songs, romance novels, and sappy movies, littered with sweet lyrics and poetic words that our hearts cling to like a bee to honey. The media creates a world where our feet never touch the ground, our lives smell like roses, and our vision is perfect as we look through our rose-colored glasses. Do not misunderstand me—during some seasons in our lives and throughout our experiences, we are over the moon, and we see the shimmering pot of gold at the end of the rainbow. However, more often than not, those occasions will be few and far between. Then what?

Truth be told, loving is hard work, messy, and intentional. There is that word again: intentional, it is a choice. I think that is why one of the fruit of the Holy Spirit is long-suffering because, from the onset, God is setting the stage for us. Life will come at us, and at times, it will take no prisoners. In that place of difficulty, when the marriage appears to be over, the teenager is escaping to the abyss of drugs and cutting, the boss belittles you in front of the whole office, or the best friend shares your intimate secret with the Bible study group, love seems empty and hollow.

Love wanes when God's promises are delayed, when the cancer returns, when the long-awaited pregnancy ends in miscarriage, when expectations are not met. What should we do? We choose. We choose to love. Period. I know for certain that this is easier said than done when the fairy tales says that you ride off into the sunset and live happily ever after. But God made hard choices too. He chose to love, and because of that incredible and relentless love, he sent his precious Son, Jesus, as an example.

Perhaps at this moment, the thought is creeping in that it is easy for God because he's God and supernatural. But you and I are human. Think about how much easier it would have been for God to go back to the drawing board and start all over. He did it once, and he can do it again. He did not even consider that option as we see from Genesis 3:15. His plan was that Eve's offspring would bear the responsibility of reconciling us back to him.

While at a ladies' retreat a number of years ago, I received such a clear picture of the cross. God sent Jesus to the cross for you and me, but Jesus' love for you and me kept him there. The next thought that settled in my heart changed me forever. I heard that still, small voice that whispered ever so gently, "At the cross, I showed you that I was loving you into greatness." He made his choice; he chose to love me and you into greatness.

What about you? Who do you need to love into greatness?

Prayer: *Dear heavenly Father, just as Jesus chose love on the cross, I choose to love today with intentionality. I ask that you rewrite the definition of love in my heart and I would be brave to daily walk it out in my life. I repent of any thoughts rooted in selfishness that do not allow the Holy Spirit to move freely to bring about change in my life. Lord, I ask that I see as you see and that I would choose to love this broken world like you have loved me. I pray that I am sensitive to your promptings to deal in love with my family, my friends, my church, my job, and my community, especially when it is difficult to do so. Jesus, help me to operate from a place of love, especially toward the person who is the hardest to love. Amen.*

STEPS I CAN TAKE TO BECOME MORE LOVING

1.

2.

3.

Scripture ON BEING LOVING

- And over all virtues put on love, which binds them all together in perfect unity. ~ *Colossians 3:14*
- Do everything in love. ~ *1 Corinthians 16:14*

Week One

Week two

Week three

Week Four

ATTITUDE #3

be authentic

This above all: To thine own self be true, and it must follow, as the night the day, thou canst not then be false to any man.

— "HAMLET," SHAKESPEARE

Many of us spend time daily scrolling through our Facebook newsfeed, Instagram stories, and Pinterest posts. If we are honest, we sometimes find ourselves wishing we were the ones basking on a sandy beach or giving a closet tour in our dream home. Thoughts of comparison permeate our minds and weigh down our hearts. We are constantly comparing our daily grind to a two-minute highlight reel from a friend or even a stranger. If we were privy to the behind-the-scenes action of that structured setting or heavenly backdrop, we might glimpse some special lighting fixtures, carefully arranged vignettes, or sophisticated camera equipment. At times, experts with trained eyes might capture the perfect shot or use the latest high-tech software with the newest filters to masquerade all sorts of imperfections. In other words, it is not real at all.

Whether material or immaterial, most people prefer the real deal: real cheese, not artificial; real diamonds, not cubic zirconia; or an artist's real voice, not synthesized noise. Real wins out almost every time. Authenticity means the whole you, flaws and all. It means celebrating your strengths as they empower you and confronting your weaknesses as they challenge you. It means not being afraid to embrace vulnerability.

It is okay to want to change and be a better version of yourself if the standard you measure yourself against is Jesus. His reflection and his love for you will weed out the false and reveal the true authentic you he created you to be.

The Bible story of Gideon addresses authenticity and is found in Judges 6–8. The odds were stacked against him, or so he thought. He was hiding behind the threshing floor in the dark, trying to escape detection and to remain insignificant because of who he thought he was. Then the angel of the Lord appeared, confronting him boldly and loudly. Read Gideon's response or, really, his excuse in Judges 6:15. "My clan is the weakest in the whole tribe of Manasseh, and I am the least in my entire family!" (NLT).

God was not about to let Gideon off the hook, so the excuse did not work. God confronted Gideon's excuse so that it would not hold him back. Under the cloak of darkness, the angel declared how God saw Gideon and what he was created to do. At that moment, in the stillness of the night, God revealed to Gideon his true, authentic self. He was not a coward; he was not created to be full of fear. But God created him to be a warrior, a warrior not of a huge, substantial army but of an army small in number yet big in backing. God would be with Gideon and his army so that God would get the glory.

The first step in living a truly authentic life is to just believe as Gideon did. After securing God's total approval, Gideon believed. He believed before he saw. He captured God's vision of who he was through the angel. He clung to that to lead his warriors into victory. So many people in our world would rather risk losing themselves by living a fake persona then walk around in their authenticity.

One of the best quotes that has helped me in my journey toward authenticity is this: "It is better to fail in originality than to succeed in imitation." [2]

What about you? Do you struggle with being authentic? Do you make excuses — fear, lack of knowledge, lack of resources, negative words spoken over you—for not leading an authentic life?

____

____

____

Prayer: *Dear heavenly Father, I long to be authentic in this world. I mentally, emotionally, and spiritually grasp hold of your heart for me. Let me catch a glimpse of the destiny you breathed into me while you formed and shaped me in my mother's womb. God, I repent for comparing myself with others and only focusing on my shortcomings. I ask that I fulfill the call you have set before me with an authenticity and uniqueness as you desire for me. Amen.*

STEPS I CAN TAKE TO BECOME MORE AUTHENTIC

1. ______________________________

____

2. ______________________________

____

3. ______________________________

____

Scripture ON BEING AUTHENTIC

- Let love be genuine. Abhor what is evil; hold fast to what is good. ~ *Romans 12:9*

Week One

Week two

Week three

Week Four

ATTITUDE #4

be hopeful

Hope is the things with feathers that perches in the soul and sings tunes without the words and never stops at all.

— EMILY DICKINSON

We must accept finite disappointment but never lose infinite hope.

— MARTIN LUTHER KING JR.

As I sit to write this month's devotional topic, our world has been thrust into the worst pandemic it has encountered in more than one hundred years. I am very cognizant of the fact that today, more than ever, humanity is in need of hope. Believers and unbelievers alike are grappling with fears of this health crisis, job loss, social isolation, and depression, just to name a few. Never before have we had so much in common with our global neighbors as we do now in combatting this epidemic. However, the greatest necessity is for Jesus, our hope in times of trouble.

The apostle Paul, in 1 Corinthians 13, considers hope one of the trifectas required for pilgrimage on our Christian travels in this life. To me, hope comes as a soothing salve, not only providing healing but offering comfort and protection during the darkest of times. After losing our baby boy shortly after childbirth, I struggled for several years with a fractured faith because my anchor of hope wavered in the waters of discouragement and loss. The question was not if Jesus was near in my time of trouble, but what his plan was to bring healing from all this pain for me and my family. I mentally understood that his promises were "yes and amen," yet when would he step into all the broken places of our family?

As time dragged on and my precious tribe endured loss after loss, my hope diminished to the point that I felt as though I were slowly edging toward that dark pit of depression. I knew I needed to dig deep spiritually to see where I had lost my way. Through prayer, reflection, and Bible searching, I came across two passages that highlighted all I was going through. One of those was Proverbs 13:12. "Hope deferred makes a heart sick, but a longing fulfilled is a tree of life" (NIV).

Hebrews 6:18–19 says, "God did this so that, by two unchangeable things in which it is impossible for God to lie, we who have fled to take hold of the hope set before us may be greatly encouraged. We have this hope as an anchor for the soul, firm and secure. It enters the inner sanctuary behind the curtain" (NIV).

I envisioned Proverbs 13:12 as a spiritual mountain: One side was hope deferred, and I was ascending it at a snail's pace. The mountain peak in its full panoramic view with all the splendor of my dream of a son stretched out before me. Yet as quickly as he came, he left, leaving such a void. I yearned to make sense of such a senseless tragedy. How would God use this for his glory? I was stuck, trying to wrap my finite mind around the ways of an infinite Creator. It was hopeless and impossible.

During my grief, I heard that the loss of a parent is your past, the loss of a spouse is your present, and the loss of your child is your future. I could not agree more, for even while pregnant, I felt as if I had lived a lifetime already with my sweet boy. What would I do now with all the space and plans in my heart of this precious wanted child? The shift happened when I chose to renew my hope in Jesus and fully released that dream to be a mom to my little boy.

Letting go and trusting in God is foundational to restoring hope and breathing life back into your spiritual lungs, which propels you forward to dream again. Letting go is the crucial link that moves you away from the jagged shoreline of unfulfilled desires into the deep, unchartered ocean of God's amazing blueprint for your life. Trust is the compass that navigates and positions you to receive all that God had envisioned for you. Hope anchors you securely in the midst of it all, whether the calm, still waters of peace or the turbulent storms of despair. That is where we are met by the one who sees and knows it all.

What about you? Have you been feeling hopeless? Have you been feeling hopeful?

Prayer : *Dear heavenly Father, I ask that you help me to hold unto hope, even when I do not understand. I pray I can lean on you to renew my hope and trust. Set me back on the course you intended for me. May I be able to rest under the shadow of your wings and restore my longings, according to your riches and glory. May I be brave enough to let go of all the disappointments and fears that have kept my hopes deferred, and may I step forward in full confidence, knowing you are my strength, my refuge, and strong tower. Dig deep, Holy Spirit, and awaken those areas that have lain dormant for so long because of deferred hope. Amen.*

STEPS I CAN TAKE TO BECOME HOPEFUL

1.

2.

3.

Scripture ON HOPE

- And You will be secure, because there is hope; you will look about you and take your rest in safety. ~ *Job 11:18 (NIV)*

Week One

Week two

Week three

Week Four

be content

To be content doesn't mean you don't desire more, it means you're thankful for you have and patient for what's to come.

— TONY GASKINS

I once heard that contentment is an art form; in other words, it is a skill you must learn and practice. To a certain extent, I agree, because, for the most part, it is not something that comes naturally to people. Maybe you have been around a couple of toddlers, and you handed a toy to one. Then you gave another toy to his friend, only to see the first child discard his toy and begin a tug-of-war battle over the second toy.

As adults, I do not think we outgrow that attitude unless we are intentional and focused. If you live in the United States, a couple of common sayings express this. "The grass is always greener on the other side of the fence." "Keeping up with the Jones'" means that we are trying to keep up with the material possessions of others: whatever is better, bigger, newer, or more special than what we have.

If we are honest, then that is true. Someone else will always be prettier, smarter, richer, or more than we are, so we need to start there. However, it should not matter because we were not called to walk in their shoes; we were called to walk our own path.

Learning to be content means being satisfied or having peace of mind, no matter your lot in life. You are learning to just be you, and you should be okay with that. This is the starting point. You have survived all of your worst days in spite of yourself. This is evidence of God's grace and goodness toward you.

You don't need to look to the left or the right, to someone else to use as a gauge as to how successful or blessed you are. This is crucial to the art of contentment. I have read many articles or social media posts about someone who seemingly has it all, but when that same person opens up, they reveal how truly empty, insignificant, and lonely they honestly feel. Here we are, trying to emulate them while feeling so irrelevant, when our supposed role model is not even content with who they are or what they have.

Emotions drive us so that we are jumping through hoops, running, and dodging obstacles, all in the name of achieving something—anything!—just as long it is not what we currently have. There is nothing wrong with having goals, ambitions, or role models to motivate us to improve ourselves. But we need to look at the why behind it all. Wanting better is not the problem; it is figuring out the motivation behind it all.

If we are driven by self-loathing and fear, then no amount of change will help us. All of us have areas that need improvement, and we should embrace our strengths and our weaknesses to become a better version of ourselves. The difference is when we welcome God and live from a place of contentment. This takes the pressure off so that we don't think, *I will feel better about myself when I do this or that. I will love myself when I have accomplished this or that.*

Life is littered with people who, in their drive to succeed, become discontented and turn their lives to shambles. Discontentedness is not content (pun intended) with just stopping there. No, you can well expect that along with it, will come its evil stepsiblings: envy and jealousy. Without a doubt, we open a door in our hearts when we choose not to live in contentment. Contentment is like a river that flows and captures with it peace, joy, and hope as it courses over the peaks and valleys of our lives. It buffers us against self-destructive thoughts and behaviors when we choose to look at life through the perspective of a glass half full and not half empty.

You may be inclined to put this devotional down right about now in annoyance or with thoughts of *Oh, brother, is she for real with this glass half full garbage?* Oh, I get it, trust me! And for most of my life, I was that person who would roll my eyes when anyone shared their rosy perspective. I seriously wanted to slap someone or stand up and shout, "Give me a break." Do not worry, by God's grace, I never acted on those thoughts. However, I began shifting my mindset as my relationship grew deeper with the Lord. I opened myself up to his immeasurable love for me, even as I listened to the song, "Reckless Love."

I was always looking at what I lacked, never leaving room for what I already had. I was always looking at how far I had to go and not how far I had come, seeing what I had yet to achieve and not what I had already overcome. Once I broke free of those patterns, then and only then, did I begin to understand the significance of being content. When someone understands contentment through God's perspective, they will be compelled to continue to give or bless an individual who is chronically discontented.

Now God is not vindictive, but he is wise because he sees that more doesn't equal better. In other words, a person won't get better in their heart simply by possessing more of anything: wealth, health, talents, gifts, etc. Contentment is like a funnel directly depositing in us a need to view everything through the lens of grace. We learn good stewardship, regardless of how much or how little. Wow, what a gift we have been given.

The story of Cain and Abel comes to mind here. Most of us have heard of the infamous narrative of one brother murdering the other, the inception of humanity's sibling rivalry. An epic and sad melodrama rolled up into one as one brother feels rejection while the other basks in recognition. Reading the story, one almost feels sorry for Cain because of the rejection, but here is the catch in Genesis 4:7. "If you do what is right, will you not be accepted? But if you do not do what is right, sin is crouching at your door; it desires to have you, but you must rule over it" (NIV).

Here, we clearly see God was not playing favorites; God saw Cain's heart but went a step further and warned him of what would come if that sin was allowed to reign. The dispute was not whether Abel was better or more worthy than Cain; it is what Cain believed. He chose to see something that was not there, and he behaved accordingly. In his mind, God must've accepted Abel more; therefore God loved him better than he loved Cain. This bitter cycle is perpetual when we allow our hearts to go unchecked. As the warning from the beginning of creation predicted, sin crouches with its desire. That desire will destroy our hearts if we do not master it.

What about you? Do you find yourself always looking at what others have or desiring what they are doing? Is it hard for you to be happy when others are blessed? Do you see yourself as a contented person?

Prayer: *Dear heavenly Father, I repent and confess that I have acted out of discontentedness. Please forgive me for grumbling and complaining about what you have entrusted to me. I am sorry for entertaining thoughts that have led me to be envious or jealous of others and for choosing not to properly steward what you have placed in my life. Lord, help me to live from a heart of contentment and gratitude for all the opportunities and blessings you have provided. Teach me to guard my heart from the enemy's plot and distractions. Keep me from coveting what my neighbor has so that I can yield myself to you. Amen.*

STEPS I CAN TAKE TO BECOME CONTENT

1.

2.

3.

Scripture ON CONTENTMENT

- Godliness with contentment is great gain. For we brought nothing into the world, we can take nothing out of it.
  ~ 1 Timothy 6:6–7

Week One

Week two

Week three

Week Four

ATTITUDE #6

be present

If you look back, do so forgivingly. If you must look forward, do so prayerfully. However, the wisest thing you can do is to be present in the present. Gratefully.

— MAYA ANGELOU

While on vacation a number of years ago in Savannah, I witnessed the most interesting scene. Cruising up the cobblestone street was a hearse, and in lieu of a cargo area, a couple of rows of seats carried not a coffin but a group of tourists. I thought, *What a curious way to view the historic streets of this beautiful southern city, from the back of vehicle defined by death and sorrow.* Such a metaphor of life, I suppose. How many of us have trouble being present in our daily lives because we are too busy reflecting on our past? We are tethered to our past mistakes, obsessed with the "woulda, coulda, and shoulda" scenarios dancing around our heads that keep us from focusing on the here and now.

Perhaps the past is not the problem but the future—the fear of the unknown, the "what ifs," and the maybes—causing us to now suffer from analysis paralysis. Jesus knew how the minds of people worked, so he addressed the topic in the beautifully stated passage in Matthew 6. The Son of Man exposed the elephant in the room and the related emotions when we continually live in the past or future, overlooking the present. Jesus identified what announced itself at the door of our hearts—worry, that consistent and persistent angst and uneasiness, vying for prominence in our hearts and cluttering our minds. Worry creates noise, a disturbance that prevents us from hearing clearly from God and resting in his peace.

The Teacher provided the solution when he said, "Stop worrying. Be present." He also reminded us that God would take care of us. The Son of God modeled this very mentality till the end. Who better than Jesus had reason to be the epitome of a worrier, right? He was surrounded by fickle disciples, throngs of people with demanding needs, a betrayer in his midst, zealots out for blood, and an impending date with death. How much more should he have been curled up in a corner, biting his nails, wallowing in self-pity? Yet he was not. He reminded himself that his heavenly Father promised to provide for his every need. If he did it for the birds of the air and flowers in the field, how much more so would he do so for his Son? (See Matthew 6:26–27.)

In other words, live by the following mottos:

- ✓ Live for today.
- ✓ Forget about the past because you cannot change it.
- ✓ Postpone thinking about the future for it will bear enough trouble when it comes.
- ✓ Be present today.

I used to pride myself on being a wonderful multi-tasker. Becoming a mom catapults you into a realm where you morph into this superhuman with eyes in the back of your head, limbs covering all sides of your body, and feet that can carry you as swiftly and gracefully as a gazelle. I never mastered the graceful part, but I did feel as though I had to have all these moving parts while carrying out everything with precision to keep the littles safe, the home organized, the job secured, and the activities going. These are all a necessary part of parenting; however, I sometimes forgot to stop and smell the coffee, to check in with my kiddos at the very moment they needed me most. That's because I was trying to juggle all the plates of my life and keep them from crashing down and breaking.

Living that way meant details went unnoticed, feelings were overlooked, and opportunities were missed time and time again. For me, dealing with worry meant I tried to control everything and everyone. If I could control it, then life would feel secure, stable, safe, and predictable. We all know what a fallacy that is. We really are not superhuman; we are fallible, flawed, and frivolous. Only through Christ and through daily surrender to him—yielding our wills, releasing the worry, and abiding in the present—can we experience the certainty Jesus described and lived out in Matthew 6.

What about you? Do you struggle with living in the present? Does worry distract you?

____

____

____

____

____

Prayer: *Dear heavenly Father, I ask you to teach me how to remain in the present. Help me place all control and worry at the feet of Jesus. May I daily remember that God's promises are true and he is faithful to his Word. I believe that just as God is a God of detail and remembers the sparrows and the lilies, how much more will he remember me? With your help, Father, may I consistently practice being present with my family, friends, and co-workers so I can soak in the special moments and experiences we have together. Amen.*

STEPS I CAN TAKE TO BECOME MORE PRESENT

1. ____

____

2. ____

____

3. ____

____

Scripture ON BEING PRESENT

- So, don't worry about tomorrow, for tomorrow will bring its own worries. Today's trouble is enough for today.
  ~ Matthew 6:34 (NLT)

Week One

Week two

Week three

Week Four

ATTITUDE #7

be an overcomer

Success is not measured by wins and losses but by how you overcome all of what life's tosses.

— ZACHARY CORROTHERS

One of my favorite people in history is, hands down, Winston Churchill. Yep, the one, the only, out-spoken, resilient, and larger-than-life personality who, without question, left his mark on this planet. Churchill was born into a life of privilege, rarely seen by his absentee mother, and reared by nannies and educators at multiple boarding schools. His was a life imprinted by countless rejections, both personally and professionally, and yet from an early age, his tenacity and fierce independence saw Churchill conquer many obstacles. Winston's pivotal role during World War II sealed his fate in history, bringing his country fame against a powerful adversary. In spite of his failures and shortcomings, he overcame many obstacles.[3]

Another one of my favorite historical figures is a prominent man in the Bible, King David. He was bestowed with one of the best compliments ever given—by God himself, no less. God described him as "a man after my own heart," but David's story could have had a quite different ending except for one thing. David knew and believed God; he spent hours in solitary settings, entertaining an audience of one. This unlikely choice for a king captured God's heart because David's greatest desire was to know God and be known by him and him alone.

Imagine the setting. His mother, father, who was Jesse, and some of his siblings welcomed the prophet Samuel in David's living room, as told in 1 Samuel 16. Overlooked by his whole family, the lowly shepherd waited in the fields, attending his sheep and standing ready to kill any predator that drew near. Meanwhile, back at home, excitement and suspense filled the air, as all wondered what honor brought Samuel to their threshold. I can just imagine the twinkle in Jesse's eyes and the tingle in his ears as the words rolled off the prophet's tongue. "The future king of Israel." How the thoughts must have danced around these proud parents' minds. The oldest, of course, or if not him, perhaps the strongest. Or maybe the smartest, but never the youngest. Certainly not him. That living room encounter set the tone throughout David's life of being overlooked time and time again. But here is the thing—the big but. God never overlooked David, as he told Samuel in 1 Samuel 16:7. "For the Lord sees not as man sees: man looks on the outward appearance, but the Lord looks on the heart"

You might be wondering what rejection or being overlooked has to do with overcoming. These feelings lay a foundation for many hearts to surrender or give up on what God has created or called them to do. The weight of the words spoken over you by a parent, teacher, boss, child, or family member (the list can go on and on) can paralyze or handicap you to such a degree that you stay stuck. You are right where you started. It's as if you were swallowed up by quicksand or tethered to a wall. It is not supposed to be that way, but God sees the heart and knows you. He held your destiny in the palm of his hand when you were created, and you were created to overcome. You have been equipped with all the gifts and talents you need to move forward.

What about you? Do you feel as if life has overcome you? Do you feel stuck in limbo? Or do you feel as though, with God's help, you are overcoming?

____

____

____

____

____

____

Prayer: Dear heavenly Father, thank you that you have created me to be an overcomer. In your Word, you declare that I am the head and not the tail and that no weapon formed against me will prosper. I stand with my full armor against the fiery darts of the enemy. I find myself in you, my fortress and my rock. May I view the struggles of life as a refining of my character so that the gold comes forth. Amen.

STEPS I CAN TAKE TO BECOME AN OVERCOMER

1. ______________________________

____

2. ______________________________

____

3. ______________________________

____

Scripture ON BEING AN OVERCOMER

- In all these things we are more than conquerors through him who loved us. ~ *Romans 8:37 (NIV)*
- And the Lord will make you the head and not the tail, and you shall only go up and not down, if you obey the commandments of the Lord your God, which I command you today, being careful to do them. ~ *Deuteronomy 28:13*

Week One

Week two

Week three

Week Four

be teachable

Our acute need is to cultivate a willingness to learn and to remain teachable.

— CHARLES SWINDOLL

A popular Christian song speaks of having wonder. In fact, one of the lines invites the listener to ask God to fill us with awe and wonder. The first time I heard the song, I immediately thought of children. If you have ever been around a child, even briefly, you are exposed to the beauty of wonder. They are filled with questions, and when they receive some of those answers, their eyes widen, and a smile spreads across their faces. Those signs reveal the grasp of the "aha" moment of wonder.

God created us to marvel in that wonder. It suggests an openness to being teachable, an openness to learning things we have never seen, heard, or experienced, things that may be hard to understand. But with time and patience, we will come to comprehend them. It might be teaching a Bible study, learning a new skill, or seeing a new place. No matter your age or background, having a teachable attitude will uncover a world full of inspiration and awe.

The story of the rich young ruler comes to mind in Matthew 19:16–22. A rich young man approached Jesus, a teacher he was eager to learn from. He questioned Jesus about obtaining eternal life. He was probably secretly pleased with himself because he felt he had already checked off all the to-do boxes. However, he fell short in one requirement; he was asked to leave it all behind and follow Jesus. In other words, Jesus was saying to him, "Come follow me. Let me teach you. Come learn from me all you need to know about eternal life and so much more."

The Bible says the rich young ruler walked away grieved; his pride and excuses would not let him be taught by the one who desired to share the heavenly mystery. A teachable heart comes at a price. It means releasing what keeps us from fulfilling the teachable moments in our lives that God has laid out before us.

A teachable spirit walks hand in hand with the beauty of humility. Our world applauds being first instead of last, no matter the cost, being a leader instead of a servant, and being forceful instead of willing. Humility lends itself to a yielding, a surrendering of oneself, to start at the beginning, no matter how hard or long. It means passing opportunities to get ahead of the next guy if it means cutting corners or taking shortcuts. As my friend used to always say when people asked why she was not in a hurry, "Slow and steady wins the race."

Recently, I heard of a man who had gained international fame, and one of his strongest attributes was being teachable. At the age of forty-eight, Carl Allamby fulfilled a childhood dream and became a doctor. He grew up in an impoverished community in East Cleveland with little hope of ever achieving his aspiration. So he settled on becoming a car doctor and was the best one in his area, running a successful auto shop for fifteen years.[4]

Then the longing began, but this time, he would fulfill that longing by enrolling in college to obtain a business degree. Unbeknownst to him, Carl was required to take a biology class. He found that bewildering, yet there he sat. As they say, the rest is history. That spark was once again ignited as he answered the soft whisper of his childhood dreams. Today, he is an ER resident at a university hospital in Ohio. Did his years of being a mechanic go to waste? Nope, not according to his colleagues. This is part of what makes Dr. Carl Allamby an incredible doctor. Those years taught him to have exceptional customer service skills, which he now uses on his patients.[5]

What about you? Is there an area in your life where you need to be teachable?

____

____

____

Prayer: Dear heavenly Father, may I desire a teachable, humble spirit, and may I look to your precious Son, Jesus, as the supreme example. May I lay at your feet every lofty thought and ambition that would cause me to be proud and unyielding. Lord, I ask that I learn to love your wisdom and truth and diligently seek to apply these to all areas of my life. Father, I pray that when you look down from your glorious throne that you see a heart fully prepared to be discipled, trained, and taught. Amen.

STEPS I CAN TAKE TO BECOME MORE TEACHABLE

1. ______________________________

____

2. ______________________________

____

3. ______________________________

____

Scripture ON A TEACHABLE SPIRIT

- Poverty and disgrace come to him who ignores instruction, but whoever heeds reproof is honored. ~ *Proverbs 13:18 (ESV)*

Week One

Week two

Week three

Week Four

ATTITUDE #9

be humble and meek

True humility is not thinking less of yourself;
it's thinking of yourself less.

— RICK WARREN

The virtue of humility (bless its heart) sometimes receives a bad rap. You rarely hear it mentioned in the laundry list of attractive qualities when someone describes the spouse they are looking for. It is never mentioned as a job requirement by employers. Yet humility is a spiritual principle that God seeks in the lives of his children. Over and over again, throughout the Bible, we read Scriptures and stories revealing the importance of humility for the heart of a believer. Truthfully, I think the mere mention of describing a humble person conjures up thoughts of a person who is weak, powerless, or tame. But after spending any amount of time in the presence of God and diving deep into his Word, wow. We can see the polar opposite: An individual must possess much strength to operate daily in this fallen world with a spirit of humility or meekness. The human heart, by nature, is inclined to seek exaltation more readily than modesty, to elevate self over others, to self-promote in an effort to validate who we are and what we do. Our identity quite comfortably snuggles into a place where we can seek to exalt ourselves rather than humble ourselves.

Humility begins with the condition of one's heart, period. It requires a true self-examination under the magnifying glass of the Holy Spirit to reveal the root behind our actions. Sometimes even our singular attempts at humility can, in fact, be our need to feel superior. These masquerade as false humility. Humility relates more with how we view ourselves while meekness reveals how we view others. The word "meek" derives from the Greek word in the New Testament, praus, meaning, "strength brought under control." [6]

Jesus exhibited both traits while here on earth. In the revelation of the person of Jesus, we find the best and truest example of a humble servant. He continuously and tirelessly served and submitted to the needs and the authority of others without complaint.

One of the most profound and beautiful acts of yielding himself plays out at the Last Supper, the setting somber, the scene illuminating the intimacy Jesus had established with his disciples. Foremost in Jesus' mind was the evidentiary fact that, in spite of three close years with this band of brothers, all would desert him in just a matter of hours. How did Jesus, the king and lord of all, choose to spend his final hours with them? By humbly wrapping a towel around his waist and, with meekness, washing the feet of those who would not only abandon him but who would sell him for thirty pieces of silver. Jesus sets the standard, showing us that it is not only possible but necessary to grasp hold of the attributes of humility and meekness for our Christian journey. We cannot overcome feelings of grandeur, self-righteousness, and envy apart from humility and meekness. Matthew 5:5 puts it like this: "Blessed are the meek, for they shall inherit the earth."

Jesus demonstrated such bridled strength, completely submitted to his heavenly Father. He could look past the future betrayal, the reckless abandonment by others, and blatant denial. He held steadfast to the "joy laid before him" to see that these wavering companions would one day realize their humble worth and change the world forever. There's hope for all of us yet.

What about you? Do you struggle with humility and meekness? Can you see areas of your life where you need to be more humble or meek?

Prayer: Dear heavenly Father, create in me the same heart Jesus showed at the Last Supper, one of humility and meekness. Lord, I lay down all pride and self-promotion to serve others at home, church, and throughout my community. May I see humility as you see it, Father, and may I desire to develop this virtue in my character. I repent of acts and deeds I have done that reflected anything but being your humble and meek servant. Show me how to be courageous and give me the strength to believe that, through humility and meekness, I, too, can change the world around me. Amen.

STEPS I CAN TAKE TO BECOME MORE HUMBLE AND MEEK

1. ______________________________

____

2. ______________________________

____

3. ______________________________

____

Scripture ON BEING HUMBLE AND MEEK

- Humble yourselves before the Lord and he will exalt you.
  ~ James 4:12
- But I will leave within you the meek and humble. The remnant of Israel will trust in the name of the Lord.
  ~ Zephaniah 3:12 (NIV)

Week One

Week two

Week three

Week Four

ATTITUDE #10

be fearless

F-E-A-R has two meanings: Forget Everything and Run, or Face Everything and Rise. The choice is yours.

— ZIG ZIGLAR

Everything that you always wanted is on the other side of fear.

— GEORGE ADDAIR

Fear. This small four-letter word evokes the very emotion just by the mere mention of it. Only recently, have I have begun to view fear differently. I am now categorizing it by its positive and negative attributes. Deciphering the difference between a healthy fear versus an unhealthy fear can be pretty confusing. You might be wondering, right about now, how fear can be healthy or used in a positive context. Well, I believe God allows us to experience healthy fear for our protection and preservation.

Think of Joseph, Jesus' stepfather, when he was awoken by the angel, warning him of eminent danger and telling him to flee. Joseph did not allow that fear to paralyze him but moved forward at the angel's direction with the plan to leave his homeland. (I know, fear isn't mentioned in this passage, but Mary's husband must have had angst over the safety of his little family.) Proverbs 1:7 admonishes believers that the "fear of the Lord is the beginning of wisdom, but fools despise wisdom and instruction" (NIV).

Even so, I can almost hear your thoughts as you are reading this. The title of this devotional entry is "Be Fearless," and yet the entry starts with the different kinds of fear and how there is such a thing as positive fear. Let me explain. Negative fear provokes feelings of doubt, anxiety, depression, and worthlessness. It operates as an incapacitating agent to keep you from reaching goals, trying new experiences, meeting new people, or even daring to dream. It short-circuits your energy, zapping your ambitions.

On the other hand, positive fear is rooted in the wisdom of who God is. When you understand who God is, then you realize who you are in the Lord and how fearfully and wonderfully you were created (Psalm 139:14). This type of fear reminds you that apart from God, you are helpless like a lamb without a shepherd. This type of fear propels you into action, action guided by the wisdom and direction of the Holy Spirit who is teaching you and equipping you every step of the way. You begin to understand that in your weaknesses, he is made strong, and you aren't capable of accomplishing much, so you press in, knowing that this fear of the unknown, fear of the what-ifs, fear of the maybes, fear of the waiting, is all part of God's plan. This is pushing you, challenging you, and motivating you to draw close and pursue all that God has for you.

Many of God's servants were called to do what they felt entirely ill-equipped for, and yet when that fear arose, they looked right into the face of the situation with God's help and moved. They accomplished what they were created for and helped write a story they only dreamed about. They used that positive fear to become fearless. And you can do the same.

When my girls were little, they would approach me with the opportunity of some sort of experience, such as a roller coaster ride or going to a new friend's house. They would say that they did not want to do it. When I asked why not, they responded that they were afraid. I would tell them to do it afraid.

This was probably not what my girls wanted to hear, but I knew that if that negative fear continued to be an ever-present excuse in their lives, they would always miss out on opportunities that God had for them. You know what? Almost every time, each one would come and say that they had so much fun or that they were glad they had a chance to do this or that. If the outcome wasn't what they expected, I would tell them that they could chalk it up to experience and that they gained a great story to share with friends.

So friend, when you are faced with a circumstance and the voice of fear comes a-knockin', ask yourself these questions: Is what it is saying true? Is it leading me toward God or away from him? What emotions is this stirring: condemnation or conviction? Then confess. Confess the fear or thought, bring it into the light, and do not allow it to remain in the secret place or the place of shadows. It loses its effectiveness once it is exposed to the power of light. Next, pray. Pray by yourself or ask a group of faith-filled family or friends to agree with you about what to do with the fear. There's great strength in the counsel of a few advisors.

Do not go to Negative Nancy or Pessimistic Pete for help with overcoming fear. Chances are, you will come out smelling more like a trash can than like a rose. Think of Oscar the Grouch, the neighborhood's resident grump, living in a trash can on Sesame Street. Thank goodness, Big Bird did not engage much with him, or we would be watching a canary yellow bird with a face of a sour lemon. Nope, do not do it to yourself. Seek people who can see God's ability rather than man's.

Lastly, surrender it. Some of us have been walking around with an unhealthy fear for so long that it is no longer our enemy but is now our friend. We have asked God to remove it, yet it still remains. A friend once shared an ungodly fear that she struggled with. Frustrated and upset, she went before the Lord in prayer, asking God why he did not free her from it. After a bit, she clearly heard in her heart the following words. "I will free you of your enemies, not your friends." God, in his divine wisdom, revealed to her that after many years with this struggle, she had come to embrace the fear. Others began identifying her with that fear, so she grew comfortable with it. It was as though she had found a La-Z-Boy for this antagonizing entity to recline itself in a secret place in her heart. Once that revelation came, she realized, "I have been tethered to this thing." My friend acknowledged it was the enemy, confessed, prayed, and moved forward, eventually leading groups of people in their relationship with God. The enemy can effectively use this tool but understand it is even more powerful in the hands of God. Positive, healthy fear will lead you to a life of becoming fearless.

What about you? Have you become friends with a fear in your life? Is this fear keeping you from seeing God's plan or will?

Prayer: *Dear heavenly Father, I surrender all my fears that have kept me from fully engaging with your presence and kept me from fully knowing who you are and who I am in you. I invite you to enter those secret places in my heart that have entertained thoughts that are contrary to your Word. I take captive any fear that raises itself as a false imagination in my life and submit it to the obedience of your Son, Jesus. I banish fear from the throne of my heart, and I invite you, Father, to come and take your rightful place. Amen.*

STEPS I CAN TAKE TO BECOME FEARLESS

1.

2.

3.

Scripture ON BEING FEARLESS

- For God gave us not a spirit of fearfulness; but of power and love and discipline. *~ 2 Timothy 1:7 (ASV)*
- The Spirit of the Lord will rest upon Him-spirit of wisdom and of understanding, the Spirit of counsel and of might, the Spirit of knowledge and of fear of the Lord. *~ Isaiah 11:2 (NIV)*

Week One

Week two

Week three

Week Four

ATTITUDE #11

be thankful

If a fellow isn't thankful for what he's got, he isn't likely to be thankful for what's he's going to get.

— FRANK A. CLARK

Feeling gratitude and not expressing it is like wrapping a present and not giving it.

— WILLIAM ARTHUR WARD

When talk of being thankful arises, mental images crop up of cornucopias, glistening turkeys, and the sights and smells of fall in the air. Yet over and over again, as Christians, we are reminded to be thankful and to give thanks continuously. As with all the be-attitudes discussed in this devotional, cultivating a heart of thanksgiving positions us to look at what we have versus what we wish we had. Thankfulness causes us to constantly and consistently do a heart check, a true inspection of where we are at. We can then become aligned with the heart of God. Living in thanksgiving addresses the fact that we might not be where we want to be, but we are trusting God with all our hearts to direct and order our steps. Thankfulness acts as a tool, similar to a garden hoe tilling the ground of our hearts where we have allowed weeds of self, bitterness, covetousness, envy, or jealousy—to name just a few—to take root.

We can easily be thankful when the coffers are full and life is good. However, when life is a struggle and the future seems bleak, the true test of thanksgiving is on full display. Being thankful is the crossroad laid before us, beckoning us to choose the road less traveled with a destination to the land of promise and hope in Christ. It challenges us to forego the wide and cluttered road that leads to a life of living for self and godlessness.

An attitude of gratitude must be cultivated, practiced, and demonstrated daily toward not just our families and friends but, most importantly, to a hurting world that needs it the most. My family and I moved to a new town and started attending a new church after years of worshipping and serving at our former church. I knew I wanted to serve, yet I felt awkward and out of place in this new church filled with young families and millennials as I am entering the empty-nester stage.

But I chose to serve as a hospitality host, welcoming newcomers to our facilities, providing answers, and giving a thank-you gift to all new attendees on my assigned Sundays. Some say I have the gift of gab, but that is only when I feel comfortable with the people and my surroundings. I was so out of my element those first few Sundays, as if I were wearing an itchy rough wool sweater. I stood underneath that welcome tent, flushed and wanting to bolt to my car parked just across the street. Insecurity pounded in my head like a mallet, tenderizing any hope I might have had of making a difference to this body of believers.

Then, over the negative echo in my head, I sensed this still, small voice that said stop. I prayed quietly and chose to move beyond what I was feeling at the moment. I started thanking God, thanking him for providing a church where I could worship, for my opportunity to serve, and that in spite of what I was feeling, I could push myself out of my comfort zone.

A short time later, this young man, looking sheepish and lost, came strolling up the sidewalk. I immediately approached him and asked if it was his first time at church; he said it was. We engaged in small talk, and I learned his name and invited him to stop by after the service to receive his gift. To me, these all seemed like little gestures, basic simple acts of kindness to a stranger.

A few months after our encounter, this young man shared his testimony of how his first visit to our church was going to be his last. On the way to church, he decided he was going to kill himself, which he hoped would be his third and final attempt. The plan failed. Why? Because he was approached by a woman (me), then another woman (my mom) at a tent. As he shared, this remarkable man expressed that the mere fact that we noticed him, talked with him, and hugged him changed the trajectory of his life. Shortly thereafter, he learned that he was going to be a father.

Wow! What a story! I cannot help but consider how different the outcome could have been if I hadn't had a change of attitude sparked by that prayer of thanksgiving. Simple, real gratitude expands our territory and pushes the boundaries far and wide, inviting others into our world of selflessness.

What about you? Do you desire to cultivate a heart of thanksgiving? If yes, why?

____

____

____

Prayer: *Dear heavenly Father, may I live my life from a position of thankfulness for all you have done, all you have protected me from, and all you will continue to do for me. May thanksgiving be continuously on my mouth, and may my mouth speak from the abundance of my heart. As clay in the hand of the potter, God, fashion in me a heart that loves to be thankful. May I look for opportunities to walk out a life of gratitude, sharing with the world your amazing love. I come boldly before your throne with prayers of supplication and thanksgiving, knowing you, God, will meet me there. Amen.*

STEPS I CAN TAKE TO BECOME MORE THANKFUL

1. ____

____

2. ____

____

3. ____

____

Scripture ON BEING THANKFUL

- I will give thanks to you, Lord, with all my heart; I will tell of all your wonderful deeds. ~ *Psalm 9:1 (NIV)*

Week One

Week two

Week three

Week Four

ATTITUDE #12

be generous

We make a living by what we get, but we make a life by what we give.

— WINSTON CHURCHILL

Throughout my life, I have had the opportunity to meet some very generous people. My observation has been that generosity is an extension of their hearts. They have already made the decision to be generous long before the gift is given.

Another attribute of generous people is they never really expect anything in return. They experience such a feeling of joy in giving that this emotion is the blessing for the donor. In greater measure, I have recently wanted to become an even more extravagant giver. The challenge has been set and accepted to increase my generosity, not out of obligation, but out of a true desire to replicate the heart of God through this expression.

The Bible addresses the topic of generosity throughout numerous Scriptures, and Jesus lays out the greatest example of how to lead a generous life. He personified that very adjective in the most beautiful fashion by the laying down of his life. Luke 6:38 states, "Give, and it will be given to you. A good measure, pressed down, shaken together and running over, will be poured into your lap. For with the measure you use, it will be measured to you" (NIV).

Many sermons have been preached about this verse and its relationship to money; however, in context, money is not mentioned. Giving does not just involve financial gain or blessing, Luke 6 outlines the message of giving through the Sermon on the Mount. (See also Matthew 5–8.) Our lives need to parallel this model of generosity. Then and only then will we experience a life of overflow of spirit and character. We have all heard the adage that it is better to give than to receive, and in God's economy, this is entirely true. I've had the privilege of participating on some mission trips, and without a doubt, although I desired to bless them, I can say that I came back feeling more blessed by them instead. God wraps it up in a nice little bow when he says in Galatians 6:7, "Do not be deceived: God is not mocked, for whatever one sows, that will he also reap."

In the past, my biggest excuse for not becoming a generous person was that I was not wealthy. My mentality was limited to that one area of finances, but after carefully studying the Bible, I know there is more. Generosity encompasses the intangibles: our time, our love, our skills, and our talents. These do not cost a thing to share. Godly generosity invites us to look beyond our bank accounts and be willing to give all we have. In Luke 21, Jesus commended the poor widow above the rich man. Why? Because she offered more than she monetarily had. She purposed in her heart and mind to give God everything: body, mind, and soul.

It was a huge sacrifice to her. Jesus was well aware of her situation, and yet the act didn't go unnoticed by the one who mattered. God rejoices over us when we look beyond what we possess, surrender it all to him, and give all that we have.

What about you? Do you long to be an extravagant giver? What can you give that might not involve money?

Prayer: *Dear heavenly Father, no one else compares to your generosity and how you, as a good Father, give good gifts to your children. Lord, I want to pursue a generous heart and give, not just out of my overflow. I want to give when I am also in need, knowing full well you will provide for me. Father, I want to embrace your pleasure when you see the generosity of your children, which shows your heart. May I diligently look for opportunities to give not only my money but also my time and talents. Amen.*

STEPS I CAN TAKE TO BECOME AN EXTRAVAGANT GIVER

1. ____

____

2. ____

____

3. ____

____

Scripture ON BEING GENEROUS

- Each of you should give what you have decided in your heart to give, not reluctantly or under compulsion, for God loves a cheerful giver. ~ *2 Corinthians 9:7*

Week One

Week two

Week Three

Week Four

footnotes

"Marie Curie Biography," Biography.com, *A&E Television Networks*, accessed May 7, 2020, https://www.biography.com/scientist/marie-curie.

"Originality," Quote Investigator.com, accessed May 7, 2020, https://quoteinvestigator.com/2015/07/13/originality.

Herbert G. Nicholas, "Winston Churchill," *Encyclopedia Britannica*, accessed May 7, 2020, https://www.britannica.com/biography/Winston-Churchill.

Steve Hartman, "Auto Doctor Fulfills Childhood Dream and Becomes a Medical Doctor in His 40s," CBS News, August 9, 2019, https://www.cbsnews.com/news/auto-doctor-fulfills-childhood-dream-and-becomes-a-medical-doctor-in-his-40s.

Ibid.

"4239. praus," *Strong's Concordance* at Bible Hub.com, accessed May 7, 2020, https://biblehub.com/greek/4239.htm.

Made in the USA
Columbia, SC
09 December 2020